Science Yellow Pages

for Students and Teachers

from The KIDS' STUFF™ People

Incentive Publications, Inc.
Nashville, TN

Special acknowledgement is accorded to
- *Sandra Schurr and The KIDS' STUFF™ People*
  for compiling and organizing the
  materials included in this publication
- *Susan Eaddy for the cover design*
- *Sally Sharpe, Editor*

ISBN 0-86530-009-7
Library of Congress Catalog Card Number 87-82070

TABLE OF CONTENTS

GENERAL SCIENCE

PHYSICAL SCIENCE

EARTH SCIENCE

LIFE SCIENCE

GENERAL SCIENCE

LABORATORY EQUIPMENT FOR EVERY LAB

alcohol lamps
asbestos gauze pads
assorted weights
balance scales
barometers
beakers
bunsen burners
burette clamps
cheesecloth
compasses
convex lenses
corks
dissecting tools
dry cell batteries
filter paper
flasks
funnels
galvanometers
graduated cylinders
hot plates
iron filings
lens holders
litmus paper
magnets
magnifying glasses

metric rulers and meter sticks
microscopes
mirrors
mortars and pestles
oven mittens
petri dishes
pipettes
probes (blunt)
razor blades
ring stands and rings
rubber tubing
safety goggles
scalpels
slides (blank and prepared)
spectroscopes
stirring rods
stopwatches
suction bulbs
test tubes, holders and clamps
thermometers
tongs
tripods
vials
wooden splints

12 IMPORTANT LABORATORY SAFETY PROCEDURES

1. Make sure that all chemicals are properly labeled and stored.
2. Be sure there is easy access to fire extinguishers, first-aid kits, fire blankets, and eye-wash stations from the laboratory.
3. Wear proper eye protection devices when participating in or observing experiments involving potential eye hazards.
4. Use heat-safety items such as safety tongs, asbestos mittens, aprons, and rubber gloves.
5. Confine long hair and loose clothing. Laboratory aprons should be worn at all times.
6. Carefully read all labels and instructions.
7. When constructing an apparatus for a chemical experiment, make sure that all connections are airtight.
8. When heating a liquid in a test tube, hold the tube with a holder.
9. When heating a solid in a test tube, place the tube in a stand and move the flame of the burner back and forth to evenly heat the contents.
10. Never point the open end of a heated test tube toward yourself or any other person.
11. Work areas, including floors and counters, should be kept dry. Never handle electrical equipment with wet hands.
12. Exercise great care in noting odors or fumes. Use a wafting motion of the hand.

PARTS OF A BALANCE

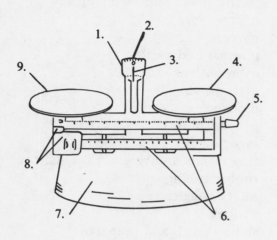

1. Scale - a graduated instrument along which the pointer moves to show if the balance is balanced
2. Zero point - the center line of the scale to which the pointer moves when the balance is balanced
3. Pointer - the marker that indicates if the balance is balanced
4. Right pan - the platform on which standard masses are placed
5. Adjustment knob - the knob used to balance the empty balance
6. Beams - scales calibrated in grams
7. Stand - the support for the balance
8. Riders - movable markers that indicate the number of grams needed to balance an object
9. Left pan - the platform on which an object whose mass is to be determined is placed

PARTS OF A COMPOUND MICROSCOPE

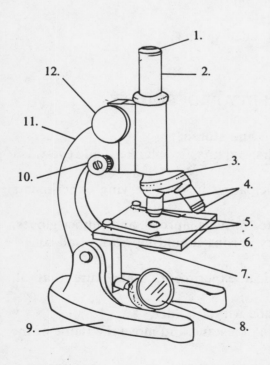

1. Eyepiece - contains the magnifying lens
2. Body tube - separates the eyepiece and the objective lenses
3. Nosepiece - holds objective lenses and can be rotated to change magnification
4. Objective lenses - a low-power lens (10x magnification) and a high-power lens (40x magnification)
5. Stage clips - hold the slide or specimen in place
6. Stage - the table on which the slide is placed
7. Diaphragm - regulates the amount of light in the body tube
8. Mirror - reflects the light upward through the diaphragm, specimen, and lenses
9. Base - supports the microscope
10. Fine adjustment knob - moves the body tube to sharpen the image
11. Arm - supports all components above the base
12. Coarse adjustment knob - moves the body tube up and down for focusing

25 SIMPLE MICROSCOPE EXPERIMENTS

1. Salt: Look for cube-shaped crystals.

2. Sugar: Look for interesting crystal shapes. Place a drop of water on the slide and watch the crystals dissolve.

3. Mold: Observe the structure of mold on bread or fruit. Leave the moldy food on a slide for one day. Note the changes that have occurred since the first observation.

4. Cloth fibers: Compare the structures of cotton, rayon, nylon, silk and polyester.

5. Fingerprints: Press a finger on carbon paper or an ink pad and then on clean paper to make a print. Examine the fingerprint.

6. Insects: Collect a variety of dead insects and study their different structures.

7. Onionskin: Peel a very thin layer from the white skin of an onion. Locate cells and examine their structure.

8. Pepper: Note the structure of pepper. Compare the magnified pepper to salt, sugar, and other spices.

9. Money: Observe the different patterns and markings of various coins and bills.

10. Hair: Compare hairs of different people and animals. Examine different colors and thicknesses.

11. Chalk: Rub a piece of chalk on sandpaper and cut a sample to make a slide. Examine the chalk dust and the sandpaper.

12. Printing: Study words printed on paper, cloth or plastic.

13. Color printing: Study different colors and patterns in colored pictures. (Comics are good for this.)

14. Crystals: Compare the crystal shapes of Epsom salts, boric acid, baking soda, bicarbonate of soda, copper sulfate, and other crystals.

15. Seeds: Collect seeds and compare their shapes, structures, and interiors.

16. Potato starch: Scrape a potato and study the starch granules.

17. Foods: Examine parts of fruits, vegetables, cereals, breads, and other foods.

18. Wood shavings: Compare wood shavings from a variety of trees.

19. Soil: Study the differences in samples of clay, sand and earth.

20. Feathers: Find and examine feathers from different birds.

21. Yarn and thread: Examine a variety of weights and textures of ribbon, rope, twine and string.

22. Rocks: Look for crystals of varying sizes in pieces of rock.

23. Water: Collect water samples after a rain from puddles, leaves and grass. Examine a drop from each surface and compare it to a drop of tap water, soapy water, salt water, etc.

24. Soap: Examine and compare shavings from different kinds of soap.

25. Iron filings: Observe several iron filings. Look for ways that they vary in size and shape.

SCIENTIFIC METHODS AND PROCESS SKILLS

To uncover facts and solve mysteries, scientists use scientific methods. There are basic steps in each method; however, the steps need not be followed in any particular order. The basic components of any scientific method include the following.

- stating the problem
- gathering information
- suggesting an answer for the problem
- performing an experiment to test the answer
- recording and analyzing the results of experiments or other observations
- stating conclusions

When following a scientific method, one uses scientific process skills such as those defined below.

1. Classifying - arranging data in a logical order

2. Communicating - exchanging information

3. Comparing - observing how things are alike or different

4. Controlling Variables - identifying and managing factors that may influence an experiment

5. Defining Operationally - listing the criteria by which something is defined

6. Experimenting - testing under controlled conditions

7. Formulating Models - devising a concrete representation to illustrate abstract relationships of objects

8. Hypothesizing - tentatively accepting an explanation as the basis for further investigation

9. Inferring - implying a conclusion from available evidence

10. Interpreting Data - finding patterns or relationships in a set of data

11. Measuring - determining magnitude in terms of the number of units

12. Observing - using the senses to obtain information

13. Predicting - foretelling from previous information

14. Questioning - raising uncertainty

15. Recording Data - gathering and systematically storing important items of information

16. Relating Time and Space - describing how position changes with time

SCIENTIFIC LAWS AND PRINCIPLES

Archimedes' Principle - the loss of weight of an object in water is equal to the weight of the displaced water

Beer's Law - a law governing the absorption of light passing through a medium; no substance is perfectly transparent, but some of the light passing through the substance is always absorbed

Beodes' Law - an empirical rule that gives the approximate relative distances of the planets from the sun

Boyle's Law - the volume of a fixed amount of gas varies inversely with the pressure of the gas

Charles' Law - the volume of a fixed amount of gas varies directly with the temperature of the gas, provided the pressure does not change

Law of Action - Newton's second law of motion; the acceleration of an object depends upon its mass and the applied force

Law of Conservation of Matter - matter is neither created nor destroyed in a chemical change, but is only rearranged

Law of Inertia - Newton's first law of motion; a mass moving at a constant velocity tends to continue moving at that velocity unless acted upon by an outside force

Law of Reaction - Newton's third law of motion; for every action there is an equal and opposite reaction

Law of Universal Gravitation - a gravitational force is present between any two objects; the size of the force depends on two factors: (1) the masses of the two objects and (2) the distance between the two objects

Newton's Law of Gravitation - all objects exert an attractive force on one another

Principle of Uniformitarianism - the processes that act on the earth's surface today are the same as the processes that have acted on the earth's surface in the past

---

SCIENTIFIC FORMULAS

Acceleration = $\dfrac{\text{Change in Velocity}}{\text{Time}}$ $a = \dfrac{\Delta v}{t}$

Density = $\dfrac{\text{Mass}}{\text{Volume}}$ $D = \dfrac{m}{v}$

Kinetic Energy = $\dfrac{\text{Mass} \times \text{Square of object's velocity}}{2}$ $Ke = \dfrac{m \times v^2}{2}$

Momentum = Mass x velocity $M = m \times v$

Potential Energy = Mass x Gravity x Height $Pe = mgh$

Power = $\dfrac{\text{Work}}{\text{Time}}$ (Force x Distance) $P = \dfrac{F \times d}{t}$

Pressure (unbalanced force) = $\dfrac{\text{Force}}{\text{Area}}$ $P = \dfrac{F}{a}$

Velocity = $\dfrac{\text{Distance}}{\text{Time}}$ (speed) $v = \dfrac{d}{t}$

Volume = Length x width x height $v = l \times w \times h$

TABLES OF MEASURE

LENGTH

Metric System
1 centimeter (cm) = 10 millimeters (mm)
1 decimeter (dm) = 10 centimeters (cm)
1 meter (m) = 10 decimeters (dm)
1 meter (m) = 100 centimeters (cm)
1 decameter (dkm) = 10 meters (m)
1 kilometer (km) = 1000 meters (m)

English System
1 foot (ft) = 12 inches (in)
1 yard (yd) = 36 inches (in)
1 yard (yd) = 3 feet (ft)
1 rod (rd) = 16½ feet (ft)
1 mile (mi) = 5280 feet (ft)
1 mile (mi) = 1760 yards (yd)

WEIGHT

Metric System
1 gram (g) = 1000 milligrams (mg)
1 kilogram (kg) = 1000 grams (g)
1 metric ton (t) = 1000 kilograms (kg)

English System
1 pound (lb) = 16 ounces (oz)
1 ton (T) = 2000 pounds (lb)

CAPACITY

Metric System
1 liter (L) = 1000 milliliters (mL)
1 decaliter (dkL) = 10 liters (L)
1 kiloliter (kL) = 1000 liters (L)

English System
1 pint (pt) = 2 cups (c)
1 quart (qt) = 2 pints (pt)
1 gallon (gal) = 4 quarts (qt)
1 peck (pk) = 8 quarts (qt)
1 bushel (bu) = 4 pecks (pk)

FAHRENHEIT AND CELSIUS SCALE

°Fahrenheit °Celsius

Normal body temperature:
98.6° Fahrenheit
37° Celsius

Boiling point of water:
212° Fahrenheit
100° Celsius

Freezing point of water:
32° Fahrenheit
0° Celsius

SELECTED SCIENTISTS AND INVENTORS

Aristotle (384 B.C. - 322 B.C.) - He was a Greek philosopher noted for his works on logic, metaphysics, ethics, and politics who was also the first to attempt a classification of animals.

Amedeo Avogadro (1776-1856) - He was an Italian physicist who discovered the molecule. A law was named after him which states that equal volumes of gases under identical conditions of temperature and pressure contain the same number of molecules.

Alexander Graham Bell (1847-1922) - He was an American inventor who invented the telephone and who became an expert in teaching deaf people to speak.

George Washington Carver (1864-1943) - He was an American botanist and chemist who discovered over 300 products that can be made from peanuts such as oil, cheese, soap, and coffee.

Nicolaus Copernicus (1473-1543) - He was a Polish astronomer who waited a lifetime before publishing his conviction that the sun, not the earth, is the center of the universe.

John Dalton (1766-1844) - He was an English chemist and physicist who is known for his atomic theory.

Charles Darwin (1809-1882) - He was an English naturalist who traced the origin of man and wrote a book titled *The Origin of Species by Means of Natural Selection*.

Thomas Alva Edison (1847-1931) - He was an American inventor who developed the electric light, the phonograph, the storage battery, the mimeograph machine, and motion pictures.

Albert Einstein (1879-1955) - He was an American physicist who discovered that mass can be changed into energy and that energy can be changed into matter. He represented this discovery with the equation $E=MC^2$. He is also known for the Theory of Relativity.

Michael Faraday (1791-1867) - He was an English scientist who was able to change electro-magnetic force into mechanical force which led to the development of the first electric generator and the electric motor.

Alexander Fleming (1881-1955) - He was an English bacteriologist who discovered that a certain mold could destroy certain types of bacteria and who consequently developed penicillin.

Henry Ford (1863-1947) - He was an American inventor who built the first gasoline engine and the first automobile. He also developed the first assembly line to speed up the production of automobiles.

Benjamin Franklin (1706-1790) - He is often referred to as the Father of American Science. By experimenting with a kite, a key, and a bolt of lightning during an electrical storm, he was able to prove that lightning and electricity are the same thing.

Galileo Galilei (1564-1642) - He was an Italian astronomer and physicist who formulated the Law of Falling Bodies and wrote about acceleration, motion and gravity. He also developed the first astronomical telescope and discovered the four moons of Jupiter.

Hippocrates (460?B.C. - 370?B.C.) - He was a Greek physician who founded the first school of medicine and, as a result, became known as the Father of Medicine.

Edward Jenner (1749-1823) - He was an English physician who founded the science of immunology by developing a vaccine to protect the body against smallpox.

Gregor Johann Mendel (1822-1884) - He was an Austrian monk and botanist who founded genetics through his work with recessive and dominant characteristics of plants.

Dmitri Ivanovich Mendeleev (1834-1907) - He was a Russian chemist who developed the periodic classification of the elements.

Sir Isaac Newton (1642-1727) - He was an English scientist and mathematician who discovered that the force of gravity is dependent upon the amount of matter in bodies and the distances between the bodies. He formulated the laws of gravity and motion and the elements of differential calculus.

Louis Pasteur (1822-1895) - He was a French chemist and bacteriologist who developed a method for destroying disease-producing bacteria and for checking the activity of furmentative bacteria (pasteurization). He developed an effective treatment for rabies.

Pythagoras (582 B.C. - 507 B.C.) - He was a Greek philosopher and mathematician who developed the Pythagorean theorem which states that the sum of the squares of the legs of a right triangle is equal to the square of the hypotenuse.

Walter Reed (1851-1902) - He was a U.S. army surgeon and bacteriologist who discovered that typhoid fever (yellow fever) was caused by a virus carried from one person to another by a mosquito.

Jonas Salk (1914-   ) - He is an American physician and bacteriologist who developed a vaccine to prevent polio.

James Watt (1736-1819) - He was a Scottish engineer and inventor who invented the modern steam engine. The "watt," a measure of electrical power, was named after him.

Eli Whitney (1765-1825) - He was an American inventor who invented the cotton gin and developed a faster way to make manufactured goods.

Orville (1871-1948) and Wilbur (1867-1912) Wright - They were the American brothers who made the first controlled and sustained airplane flight at Kitty Hawk, North Carolina on December 17, 1903.

SELECTED CAREERS IN SCIENCE

Anesthesiologist - a doctor who specializes in the administration of anesthetics or drugs to patients to induce loss of sensation or consciousness (as for surgery, etc.)

Archaeologist - one who studies the remains from past cultures in order to determine how the people of that culture lived

Astronomer - one who studies the stars, planets, and all heavenly bodies

Astrophysicist - one who studies the chemical and physical nature of objects in space

Biochemist - one who studies the chemical makeup of cells in order to determine the life processes of cells and entire organisms

Biologist - one who studies and practices the science of life processes of plants and animals

Botanist - one who studies and practices the science of botany or the study of plants

Cartographer - one who makes maps or charts

Chemical Engineer - one who applies chemistry to industrial uses

Chemist - one who studies the makeup and properties of substances and investigates how substances react with one another

Civil Engineer - one who designs and supervises the construction of highways, bridges, tunnels, waterworks, harbors, etc.

Computer Scientist - one who studies and applies the science of computer programming

Electrical Engineer - one who applies the scientific technology of electricity in such ways as the design and application of circuitry and equipment for power generation, machine control, and communications

Entomologist - one who studies insects; careers in this field include the development, production, and testing of new means of insect control and the development of alternatives to poisonous insect sprays

Environmental Analyst - one who identifies the sources of pollution by collecting and studying data concerning factories, waterways, weather, atmospheric conditions, etc.

Forester - one who is trained in the science of planting and taking care of forests, oftentimes for the production of timber, conservation, etc.

Genetic Engineer - one who applies the science of genetics through the manipulation of the genetic code in attempts to effect biological improvements in a species of animal or plant

Geologist - one who studies the structure, makeup, and history of the earth

Laboratory Technician - one who is trained to perform specific laboratory processes, tests, experiments, etc.

Medical Doctor - one who practices medicine as a general practitioner or as a specialized doctor for the treatment of sickness, injury and disease

Meteorologist - one who studies the atmosphere and the physical and chemical processes that take place in the atmosphere

Microbiologist - one who studies organisms that can be seen only with the aid of a microscope such as bacteria, molds, and viruses

Nuclear Physicist - one who studies and applies the science of physics as it deals with the structure of atomic nuclei, nuclear forces, the fission process, the study of radioactive decay, etc.

Neurologist - a doctor who specializes in the medicine dealing with the nervous system, its structure and its diseases

Nurse - one who is trained to take care of the sick, injured and aged and to assist surgeons and doctors, etc.

Oceanographer - one who studies the physical properties of the ocean such as its movements, density, and temperature is a physical oceanographer; one who studies the plants and animals that live in the ocean is a marine biologist; one who studies the ocean floor is a marine geologist

Optometrist - one who specializes in the examination of the eyes, the measurement of errors in refraction, and the prescription of glasses to correct these defects

Paleontologist - one who searches for and studies fossils; paleontologists use fossils to date rocks and to determine more about the earth and its early inhabitants

Physical Therapist - one who treats an injured or handicapped person with physical means (such as exercise, massage, heat, etc.) in order to help the patient function as normally as possible

Radiologist - one who practices the science dealing with X-rays and other forms of radiant energy used in medicine for X-raying bones and organs and for diagnosing and treating disease

Surgeon - a doctor who specializes in the treatment of disease, injury or deformity by manual or instrumental operations, such as the removal of diseased parts of tissue by cutting

Surveyor - one who measures the elevation, size and shape of any part of the earth's surface and prepares sketches, maps, and reports describing the land

Technical Writer - one who writes, contributes to, interprets, modifies, and edits technical material for manuals, resources, textbooks, etc., relating to any of the scientific industries or professions

Zoologist - one who studies the life, structure, growth, and classification of animals

TEACHER'S CHECKLIST FOR PLANNING A SCIENCE FAIR

1. Determine the main objectives of the science fair.

2. Recruit volunteers (teachers and parents) who have good organizational skills and an interest in science to serve on the science fair committee.

3. Set a time, location, and date for the science fair (schedule it to be about four to five months after the first committee meeting). Clear the date with the principal.

4. Write the science fair rules. Remember to include such things as the entry deadline, size limits for displays, requirements for final reports and logs of observations, the completion deadline, judging guidelines, and awards. Emphasize the requirement that all work be done by the student.

5. Design an entry form. Include a place for the student's name, project title, hypothesis, method, materials, and student and parent signatures.

6. Compile a list of suggested science fair topics.

7. Draft a cover letter (to be signed by the principal) which introduces the fair and explains the rules.

8. Design an evaluation form.

9. Publicize the application deadline, the date of the science fair and the awards.

10. Contact and secure judges.

11. Solicit contributions for awards and prizes.

12. Arrange a luncheon for the judges. (optional)

13. One week before the fair, send each judge a judging packet which includes the fair rules, the judging criteria, and a list of the projects to be judged in his or her area of expertise. Arrange to meet with the entire judging panel if possible.

14. Order any necessary certificates.

15. Plan and type the science fair program.

16. Plan the science fair layout. Draw a floor plan if necessary.

17. Gather all of the necessary materials and equipment such as tables, chairs, a portable address system, etc.

18. Send thank-yous to parent and teacher volunteers, judges, and demonstrators after the science fair.

30 IDEAS FOR SCIENCE FAIR INVESTIGATIONS

1. Do metals rust at different rates?

2. Does the color of the shell affect a hermit crab's choice for a home?

3. Does the temperature of the air affect the air pressure?

4. Which type of water evaporates the quickest: salt, tap, or fresh?

5. Do the different colors in the spectrum have different temperatures?

6. Do crystals grow at the same rate?

7. Does the time of day affect your body's temperature?

8. How much salt will a plant be able to tolerate and still grow?

9. Does the size of the vibration affect the loudness of the sound?

10. Which fruits contain a large quantity of acid?

11. Does color have an effect on a person's food choice? How?

12. How quickly can a mouse learn to run a maze?

13. What effect does loud noise have on growing plants?

14. Over what kind of surface can an animal carry the most weight?

15. On which road surface is the breaking surface the least?

16. Does magnetism affect an animal's behavior? How?

17. Does magnetism affect plant growth? How?

18. How do mice communicate with each other?

19. What detergent is the most biodegradable?

20. Which packaging method best reduces the growth of mold or fungus?

21. Through what surfaces does sound travel best?

22. At what time during the day does the sun give the most energy?

23. What effect does the amount of sunlight have on the color of a leaf?

24. What kind (shape) of sail will make a boat go the fastest?

25. Does gravity affect the direction that a seed grows?

26. Does the brightness of a light have an effect on the amount of heat the light produces?

27. Does a thin liquid boil faster than a thick liquid?

28. Does caffeine affect plant growth? How?

29. What surfaces reflect light best?

30. What is the highest temperature at which milk may be stored and not spoil?

STUDENT CHECKLIST FOR SCIENCE FAIR PROJECTS

_____ 1. Does your project deal with a specific problem? Do you have a hypothesis?

_____ 2. Can your question be answered through a scientific investigation?

_____ 3. Do you have a set of expectations for this investigation?

_____ 4. Have you stated your expectations before beginning the actual testing?

_____ 5. Do you have a materials and/or equipment list?

_____ 6. Have you identified the variables for your investigation?

_____ 7. Could someone else set up and conduct your investigation from your step-by-step directions?

_____ 8. Can your investigation be measured in specific units?

_____ 9. Have you taken pictures, made sketches, and/or kept a log?

_____ 10. Have you determined a table, chart or graph format?

_____ 11. Will your data allow you to draw conclusions and/or support your hypothesis?

_____ 12. Do you have a plan for accurately and creatively displaying your investigation procedure and results?

JUDGING CRITERIA FOR SCIENCE FAIR PROJECTS

1. Scientific Investigations - 40 points
   - Is the purpose/hypothesis stated on the display?
   - Is the procedure used in developing and obtaining the solution or results explained?
   - Is the method of data acquisition or analysis explained?
   - Does the data support the conclusion?

2. Creative Ability - 15 points
   - Did the student design and construct any equipment?
   - Does this project display originality?
   - Is the data presented uniquely?
   - How creative is the display?

3. Thoroughness - 20 points
   - How many times was the investigation performed?
   - Does the display physically demonstrate the operation or results?
   - Have the variables affecting the outcome been identified?
   - Are accurate amounts of materials listed?

4. Skill - 15 points
   - Is the demonstrated skill commensurate with the student's age and grade level?

5. Clarity/Neatness - 10 points
   - Is the written material clearly presented? Is the data easy to understand?
   - Is the display well-organized and attractive?
   - Is the material readable and arranged in a logical manner?

TEACHER'S ASSESSMENT CHECKLIST
FOR SCIENCE EXPERIMENTS AND PROJECTS

		Poor		Fair		Excellent
1.	Shows active participation in planned activities	1	2	3	4	5
2.	Organizes equipment and materials for experimentation	1	2	3	4	5
3.	Identifies variables before beginning experimentation	1	2	3	4	5
4.	Follows a scientific method and applies scientific process skills	1	2	3	4	5
5.	Formulates a hypothesis	1	2	3	4	5
6.	Applies observation skills	1	2	3	4	5
7.	Applies classification skills	1	2	3	4	5
8.	Records data accurately	1	2	3	4	5
9.	Demonstrates scientific curiosity	1	2	3	4	5
10.	Understands use of scientific terms and symbols	1	2	3	4	5
11.	Reads, interprets and constructs graphs and tables	1	2	3	4	5
12.	Recognizes patterns and relationships	1	2	3	4	5
13.	Predicts outcomes	1	2	3	4	5
14.	Interprets test results by synthesizing information	1	2	3	4	5
15.	Formulates reliable conclusions	1	2	3	4	5
16.	Applies problem solving techniques	1	2	3	4	5
17.	Demonstrates effective use of time	1	2	3	4	5
18.	Shows care and ability with equipment	1	2	3	4	5
19.	Follows safety precautions	1	2	3	4	5
20.	Shows care and ability in lab cleanup	1	2	3	4	5

PHYSICAL SCIENCE

STUDENT INVESTIGATIONS

1. What things make sounds?
2. How does sound travel?
3. What makes sounds differ?
4. Does sound travel in a vacuum?
5. What happens to make a thunderclap?
6. What are echoes and what causes them?
7. What kinds of materials can carry sound?
8. What is music?
9. How does light travel?
10. What is the difference between source light and reflected light?
11. From where does light come?
12. How do mirrors work?
13. How does a camera work?
14. How does the human eye work?
15. What different kinds of shadows are there?
16. Why do objects have different colors?
17. How are different colors made?
18. How is friction overcome?
19. Why do things fall?
20. How fast do objects fall?
21. What is speed, velocity, and acceleration?
22. What is the center of gravity?
23. What are the various forms of energy?
24. What happens to energy after it is used?
25. How can work be measured?
26. What is density and how does one find the density of a liquid or solid?
27. What is Archimedes' Principle?
28. What is temperature and how is it measured?
29. What is magnetism?
30. How is the earth like a magnet?
31. How can magnetism be destroyed?
32. What kinds of objects do magnets attract?
33. How can one illustrate a magnetic field?
34. How can one make a homemade compass?
35. How does electricity work for people's needs?
36. What are insulators and conductors of electricity?
37. What is an electric circuit?
38. What is Ohm's Law?
39. How does one determine which is the positive pole of a battery?
40. How does a fuse work?
41. What does the periodic table show and tell about the elements?
42. Of what are atoms composed?
43. What is the difference between a mixture and a compound?
44. What are physical and chemical changes?
45. What are chemical equations?

FORMULAS, PROPERTIES, AND USES
OF ACIDS AND BASES

Common Acids		Common Bases	
Name	**Formula**	**Name**	**Formula**
Boric Acid	H_3BO_3	Aluminum Hydroxide	$AL(OH)_3$
Carbonic Acid	H_2CO_3	Ammonium Hydroxide	NH_4OH
Hydrochloric Acid	HCl	Calcium Hydroxide	$Ca(OH)_2$
Nitric Acid	HNO_3	Potassium Hydroxide	KOH
Phosphoric Acid	H_3PO_4	Sodium Hydroxide	$NaOH$
Sulfuric Acid	H_2SO_4		

Properties of Acids	Properties of Bases
Neutralize bases	Neutralize acids
Turn litmus paper red	Turn litmus paper blue
Taste sour	Taste bitter
React with many metals to produce hydrogen	Feel slippery
Conduct electricity	Conduct electricity

Uses of Acids	Uses of Bases
water treatment	soap, glass
household cleaning products	milk of magnesia
used to etch metals and glass	mortar
used in batteries	coagulants for water purification
production of synthetic fibers	ammonia water
	lye soap

THE pH SCALE

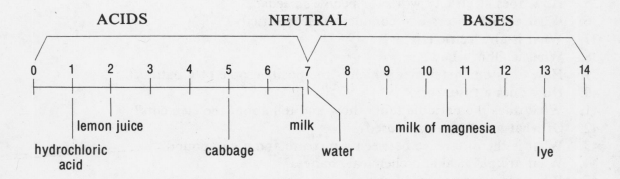

CHARACTERISTICS OF MIXTURES, COMPOUNDS, SOLUTIONS, AND SUSPENSIONS

Characteristics of Mixtures
- A mixture is made up of two or more substances which are mixed together.
- The substances in a mixture retain their individual properties.
- The substances in a mixture can be separated by physical means.
- A mixture has no definite chemical composition.
- A mixture has no chemical formula.

Characteristics of Compounds
- A compound is made up of two or more substances which are chemically combined.
- A compound has new properties unlike those of the substances that make up the compound.
- A compound can be separated only by chemical means.
- A compound has a definite chemical composition.
- A compound has a chemical formula.

Characteristics of Solutions
- A solution is a homogeneous mixture (same in structure).
- A solution is made of one or more liquid, gaseous, or solid substances dispersed in another.
- The particles in a solution dissolve.
- Solutes (substances that are dissolved in a solution) dissolve faster in a solution when they are stirred.
- Solutes dissolve faster in hot solutions than in cool solutions.
- Solutes dissolve faster in a solution when they are broken into small particles.
- A warm solvent (substance in which a solute dissolves) can usually hold more dissolved solute than a cold solvent.
- Saturated solutions contain all of the dissolved solute that they can hold.
- Unsaturated solutions can dissolve more solute.

Characteristics of Suspensions
- A suspension is a mixture of two or more substances.
- A suspension is cloudy.
- The particles in a suspension do not dissolve.
- A suspension usually settles on standing.
- A suspension can be separated by filtering.
- The particles in a suspension are larger than molecular size.

THE PERIODIC TABLE OF THE ELEMENTS

METALS

Key (example cell):

- Atomic Number: 6
- Name: Carbon
- Symbol: C
- Atomic Mass (rounded to the nearest whole number): 12
- Number of electrons in outer shell: L-4
- Outer electron shell

PERIOD	GROUP 1A	GROUP 2A	GROUP 3B	GROUP 4B	GROUP 5B	GROUP 6B	GROUP 7B	GROUP 8			PERIOD
1 Electron Shells K	**1** H Hydrogen 1 — K-1										
2 Electron Shells K-L	**3** Li Lithium 7 — L-1	**4** Be Beryllium 9 — L-2									
3 Electron Shells K-L-M	**11** Na Sodium 23 — M-1	**12** Mg Magnesium 24 — M-2									
4 Electron Shells K-L-M-N	**19** K Potassium 39 — N-1	**20** Ca Calcium 40 — N-2	**21** Sc Scandium 45 — N-2	**22** Ti Titanium 48 — N-2	**23** V Vanadium 51 — N-2	**24** Cr Chromium 52 — N-1	**25** Mn Manganese 55 — N-2	**26** Fe Iron 56 — N-2	**27** Co Cobalt 59 — N-2	**28** Ni Nickel 59 — N-2	4
5 Electron Shells K-L-M-N-O	**37** Rb Rubidium 85 — O-1	**38** Sr Strontium 88 — O-2	**39** Y Yttrium 89 — O-2	**40** Zr Zirconium 91 — O-2	**41** Nb Niobium 93 — O-1	**42** Mo Molybdenum 96 — O-1	**43** *Tc Technetium 99 — O-1	**44** Ru Ruthenium 101 — O-1	**45** Rh Rhodium 103 — O-1	**46** Pd Palladium 106 — O-1	5
6 Electron Shells K-L-M-N-O-P	**55** Cs Cesium 133 — P-1	**56** Ba Barium 137 — P-2	57-71 RARE EARTH ELEMENTS	**72** Hf Hafnium 179 — P-2	**73** Ta Tantalum 181 — P-2	**74** W Tungsten 184 — P-2	**75** Re Rhenium 186 — P-2	**76** Os Osmium 190 — P-2	**77** Ir Iridium 192 — P-2	**78** Pt Platinum 195 — P-1	6
7 Electron Shells K-L-M-N-O-P-Q	**87** Fr Francium 223 — Q-1	**88** Ra Radium 226 — Q-2	89-103 ACTINIDE SERIES	104	105	106	107				7

The names and symbols of these elements have not been assigned.

RARE EARTH ELEMENTS 57 - 71

57 La Lanthanum 139 — P-2	**58** Ce Cerium 140 — P-2	**59** Pr Praseodymium 141 — P-2	**60** Nd Neodymium 144 — P-2	**61** Pm Promethium 147 — P-2	**62** Sm Samarium 150 — P-2	**63** Eu Europium 152 — P-2	**64** Gd Gadolinium 157 — P-2

ACTINIDE SERIES 89 - 103

89 Ac Actinium 227 — Q-2	**90** Th Thorium 232 — Q-2	**91** Pa Protactinium 231 — Q-2	**92** U Uranium 238 — Q-2	**93** *Np Neptunium 237 — Q-2	**94** *Pu Plutonium 242 — Q-2	**95** *Am Americium 243 — Q-2	**96** *Cm Curium 247 — Q-2

* These elements have been made artificially.

NON-METALS

PERIOD	GROUP 3A	GROUP 4A	GROUP 5A	GROUP 6A	GROUP 7A	GROUP 0	PERIOD
1						2 **He** Helium 4　K-2	1
2	5 **B** Boron 11　L-3	6 **C** Carbon 12　L-4	7 **N** Nitrogen 14　L-5	8 **O** Oxygen 16　L-6	9 **F** Fluorine 19　L-7	10 **Ne** Neon 20　L-8	2
3	13 **Al** Aluminum 27　M-3	14 **Si** Silicon 28　M-4	15 **P** Phosphorus 31　M-5	16 **S** Sulfur 32　M-6	17 **Cl** Chlorine 35　M-7	18 **Ar** Argon 40　M-8	3

PERIOD	GROUP 1B	GROUP 2B						
4	29 **Cu** Copper 64　N-1	30 **Zn** Zinc 65　N-2	31 **Ga** Gallium 70　N-3	32 **Ge** Germanium 73　N-4	33 **As** Arsenic 75　N-5	34 **Se** Selenium 79　N-6	35 **Br** Bromine 80　N-7	36 **Kr** Krypton 84　N-8	4
5	47 **Ag** Silver 108　O-1	48 **Cd** Cadmium 112　O-2	49 **In** Indium 115　O-3	50 **Sn** Tin 119　O-4	51 **Sb** Antimony 122　O-5	52 **Te** Tellurium 128　O-6	53 **I** Iodine 127　O-7	54 **Xe** Xenon 131　O-8	5
6	79 **Au** Gold 197　P-1	80 **Hg** Mercury 201　P-2	81 **Tl** Thallium 204　P-3	82 **Pb** Lead 207　P-4	83 **Bi** Bismuth 209　P-5	84 **Po** Polonium 210　P-6	85 **At** Astatine 210　P-7	86 **Rn** Radon 222　P-8	6
7									7

65 **Tb** Terbium 159　P-2	66 **Dy** Dysprosium 163　P-2	67 **Ho** Holmium 165　P-2	68 **Er** Erbium 167　P-2	69 **Tm** Thulium 169　P-2	70 **Yb** Ytterbium 173　P-2	71 **Lu** Lutetium 175　P-2

97 ***Bk** Berkelium 249　Q-2	98 ***Cf** Californium 251　Q-2	99 ***Es** Einsteinium 254　Q-2	100 ***Fm** Fermium 253　Q-2	101 ***Md** Mendelevium 256　Q-2	102 ***No** Nobelium 254　Q-2	103 ***Lw** Lawrencium 257　Q-2

COMMON ELEMENTS AND THEIR USES

Element	Symbol	Common Uses and/or Descriptions
aluminum	Al	a light metal used in making airplanes, buildings, pots and pans, etc.
bromine	Br	used in photography, medicines, insecticides, etc.
calcium	Ca	a soft, metallic chemical element found in limestone, marble, chalk, etc.
carbon	C	found in coal, oil, gas, living things, and inks
chlorine	Cl	used in bleach, in chemicals to kill germs in swimming pools, and found with the element sodium in table salt
chromium	Cr	a shiny metal used on bumpers of some cars, household fixtures, etc.
copper	Cu	a metal used for electric wires, pots, pans, and pennies
gold	Au	a metal used for jewelry and precious decorative pieces
helium	He	a gas much lighter than air used in blimps and balloons
hydrogen	H	a flammable and explosive gas
iodine	I	used on cuts and wounds to kill germs
iron	Fe	a strong metal used in the construction of buildings, steel, and machines
lead	Pb	a metal used in automobile batteries and in fishing and diving weights
mercury	Hg	a heavy, poisonous liquid used in some thermometers
neon	Ne	a gas used in many lights and signs
nickel	Ni	a metal used in coins
nitrogen	N	the main gas in the air, also used as fertilizer
oxygen	O	a gas necessary for respiration; aids burning
platinum	Pt	an expensive metal used in jewelry
potassium	K	found in fertilizers
silicon	Si	used in electronics and in compounds for making glass
silver	Ag	used in tableware, jewelry, photography, medicines, and coins
sodium	Na	a soft metal that combines with chlorine to make table salt
sulfur	S	used to make sulfuric acid and some medicines such as pet powders
tin	Sn	used to make cans
tungsten	W	a metal used in light bulb filaments
uranium	U	a metal used in some nuclear reactions
zinc	Zn	a metal that prevents rust and is used in dry cell batteries

FLAME TESTS FOR COMMON ELEMENTS

Material to Be Tested	Element Which Makes the Color	Color of the Flame
Barium nitrate	Barium (Ba)	Yellow green
Boric acid	Boron (B)	Green
Calcium chloride	Calcium (Ca)	Orange
Copper sulfate	Copper (Cu)	Bright green
Lithium nitrate	Lithium (Li)	Dark red
Potassium dichromate	Potassium (K)	Violet
Sodium chloride	Sodium (Na)	Yellow
Strontium nitrate	Strontium (Sr)	Crimson

COMMON HYDROCARBONS AND THEIR USES

Compounds that contain only hydrogen and carbon are called hydrocarbons. Hydrocarbons may be subdivided according to the types of bonds they contain. Saturated hydrocarbons (alkanes) contain only single bonds. Unsaturated hydrocarbons (alkene or alkyne) contain double or triple bonds.

Name	Chemical Formula	Use
Butane	C_4H_{10}	Used in portable lighters, home heating fuel, portable stoves and heaters
Ethane	C_2H_6	Used to make ethyl alcohol, acetic acid, and other chemicals and also used as a refrigerant
Heptane	C_7H_{16}	Often used as a main part of turpentine
Hexane	C_6H_{14}	Used as a major part of certain motor fuels and dry cleaning solvents
Methane	CH_4	Used as a raw material for many synthetic products and as a major part of natural gas
Octane	C_8H_{18}	Used as an important part of gasoline fuel for cars, trucks, buses, etc.
Pentane	C_5H_{12}	A solvent which is commonly used as the measuring column in low-temperature thermometers
Propane	C_3H_8	Used as a "bottled gas" for home heating, portable stoves and heaters and also as a refrigerant

SIX SIMPLE MACHINES

1. **Wheel and Axle**
   A wheel and axle consists of a small wheel (the axle) attached to the center of a large wheel. When effort is applied to the wheel, the wheel and axle spreads the force over a greater distance.
   Examples: screwdrivers, doorknobs

2. **Screw**
   A screw consists of a cylindrical piece of metal threaded evenly around its outside surface with an advancing spiral ridge. Screws are basically twisting inclined planes which change the direction of force. Screws may have flat or rounded heads and pointed or flat tips.
   Examples: jar tops (with screw lids), car jacks, airplane propellers

3. **Wedge**
   A wedge is actually two inclined planes placed back to back. One end of a wedge is wide and the other end tapers to a thin edge. Wedges are used to split or cut things.
   Examples: ax, snowplow, point of a nail, pin, or thumbtack

4. **Lever**
   A lever is a bar made of a strong material which rests on a point called a fulcrum. A lever may change the direction as well as the amount of force. The three kinds of levers are pictured below.

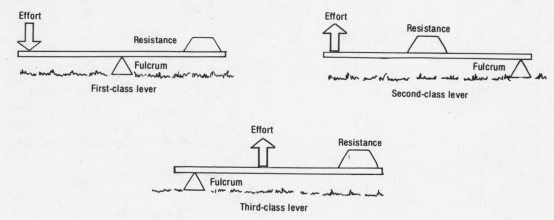

5. **Pulley**
   A pulley is a wheel with a grooved rim on which a rope moves or turns. By pulling one end of the rope, the wheel turns and lifts the load at the other end of the rope. A fixed pulley is attached to a support and does not move. A moveable pulley is attached to a load and moves as the load moves.
   Examples: flagpoles, tow trucks

6. **Inclined Plane**
   An inclined plane is a flat surface set at an angle (other than a right angle) against a horizontal surface. Inclined planes change the amount of force needed to do work. The steeper the slant, the more work it takes to go up the inclined plane.
   Example: ramps

ELECTRIC CURRENT AND THE DRY CELL BATTERY

Electric Current

Electric current is the movement of electrons through a wire. The force used to "push" the electrons along the wire is produced by a battery and is called the electromotive force. The strength of the electromotive force is measured in volts, a unit named after Alessandro Volta, the inventor of the first battery.

How A Battery Works

A battery is made up of many cells. A liquid called the electrolyte is found in each cell. This liquid is made up of billions of positive and negative charges. Two rods made of different materials are submerged in the electrolyte in each cell. These rods are called electrodes. A chemical reaction in the electrolyte sends positive particles to one electrode and negative particles to the other. When a wire is connected to the two electrodes, current flows along the wire. This current can be used to light a bulb. When the chemicals in the cell have been used up, the current no longer flows.

Parts Of A Dry Cell Battery

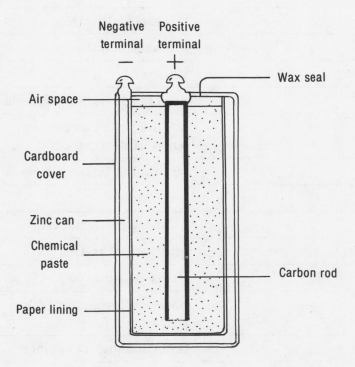

PITCH AND VOLUME SCALES

Pitch	
Frequency (Vibrations Per Second)	Examples
16	lower limit of human hearing
20-200	deep bass tones (27 = lowest note on piano)
256-512	"middle" musical scale (middle C to C above the staff)
525-3000	normal conversation
4000	about the highest musical tone
8000	high-pitched, shrill tones
20,000	upper limit of human hearing
30,000	upper limit of hearing for dogs and cats
100,000	upper limit of hearing for bats

Volume	
Decibels	Examples
0	threshold of hearing
10	ordinary breathing
11-20	whispers
21-30	ordinary household sounds
31-40	activities such as turning pages of newspapers
41-50	automobile engines & vacuum cleaners
51-60	noisy stores
61-70	ordinary conversation
71-80	heavy street traffic
81-90	trains & subways
91-100	boiler factories, air drills, riveters
101-110	thunderclaps, jet engines
120	threshold of pain

PHYSICAL SCIENCE TERMS AND DEFINITIONS

Acceleration - the rate at which the velocity of an object changes

Acid - a chemical substance that reacts with metals to release hydrogen

Atom - a tiny particle of matter consisting of a nucleus that contains protons and neutrons and an electron cloud that contains electrons

Atomic Number - the number of protons in the nucleus of an atom which identifies the kind of atom

Boiling - the process in which particles of a liquid change to gas, travel to the surface of the liquid and pass into the air

Catalyst - a substance that speeds up chemical reactions, but is not changed by the reaction

Celsius - a temperature scale used in the metric system at which water freezes at 0 degrees and boils at 100 degrees

Chemical Change - a change in which atoms and molecules form or break chemical bonds

Chemical Equation - a description of a chemical reaction using symbols and formulas

Chemical Formula - the combination of chemical symbols used as a shorthand for the name of a compound

Chemical Property - a property that describes the behavior of a substance when it reacts with other substances

Chemical Reaction - a change that produces one or more new substances

Chemical Symbol - the shorthand way of writing the name of an element

Chemistry - the study of matter

Coefficient - a number that tells how many molecules of a substance are needed or produced in a reaction

Compound - a substance made up of two or more elements

Conductor - a material that transmits or carries electricity

Conservation of Energy - the principle that energy cannot be made or destroyed, but only changed in form, and that the total energy in a physical system cannot be increased or diminished

Crystal - a solidified form of a substance in which the atoms or molecules are arranged in a definite pattern

Density - the ratio of the mass of an object to its volume

Direct Current - electric current that moves in one direction only

Electron - a negatively charged atomic particle

Emulsion - a suspension of two liquids

Fahrenheit - the temperature scale in which the freezing point of water is 32 degrees and the boiling point of water is 212 degrees

Fulcrum - the point on which a lever is supported

Galvanometer - a tool used for measuring very small electrical currents

Gas - the form of matter that has no definite shape or volume

Gravity - the force of attraction between objects and the earth

Heterogeneous Mixture - a mixture in which the composition is not the same throughout

Inertia - the property of matter to resist changes in motion

Insoluble - that which cannot be dissolved

Ion - an electrically charged atom which has lost or gained one or more electrons in a chemical reaction

Liquid - the form of matter that has a definite volume but no definite shape

Luminous Objects - objects that give off their own light

Mass - the amount of matter in an object

Matter - anything that has mass and takes up space

Mixture - a substance containing two or more ingredients which are not in fixed proportions, do not lose their individual characteristics, and can be separated by physical means

Molecule - the smallest particle of an element or compound that can exist in the free state and still retain the characteristics of the element or compound

Negative Charge - the charge of an atom having an excess of electrons (an electron has a negative charge)

Neutral - neither positively or negatively charged; neither acidic or basic

Neutron - a neutral atomic particle

Non-electrolyte - a substance that will not make water conduct electricity

Nucleus - the center of an atom which contains protons and neutrons

Oxidation - the union of a substance with oxygen; the process of increasing the positive capacity of an element or the negative capacity of an element to combine with another to form molecules; the process of removing electrons from atoms or ions

Physical Change - a change in which chemical bonds are not formed or broken and no new substance is produced

Physical Property - a property that distinguishes one type of matter from another and can be observed without changing the identity of the substance

Physics - the study of different forms of energy

Positive Charge - the charge of an atom having an excess of protons (protons have a positive charge)

Precipitate - an undissolved solid that usually sinks to the bottom of a mixture

Property - a quality that describes or characterizes an object

Proton - a positively charged particle found in the nucleus of an atom

Pure Substance - a substance that contains only one kind of material, has definite properties, and is the same throughout

Refraction - the bending of light as it passes from one medium to another

Suspension - a cloudy mixture of two or more substances that settles on standing

EARTH SCIENCE

STUDENT INVESTIGATIONS

1. What are the four "layers" of the earth?
2. What is the "inside" of the earth like?
3. What is a topographic map?
4. How are igneous, sedimentary, and metamorphic rocks formed?
5. What are some common minerals?
6. How are crystals formed?
7. How can one identify a mineral?
8. Why is it important to study minerals?
9. How do winds and waves change the earth's surface?
10. What land shapes can be formed by running water?
11. What causes earthquakes?
12. What causes a volcano to erupt?
13. How might one describe plains, plateaus, and mountains?
14. What factors affect weathering?
15. How does the soil of various climates differ?
16. How can one learn about the earth's past through observation?
17. What are fossils and how are they formed?
18. What is the geologic time scale?
19. What is the water cycle?
20. What is hydrology?
21. What is known about the gases in the air?
22. What is air pressure and how is it measured?
23. What happens to make it rain?
24. How is fog formed?
25. How can one accurately record daily weather conditions?
26. What are the different kinds of clouds?
27. What are clouds made of and how are they formed?
28. How does weather affect the earth and its inhabitants?
29. How does one read a weather map?
30. What factors determine climate?
31. How are climates classified?
32. How is relative humidity measured?
33. What are the different ways that oceans may be studied?
34. What causes ocean currents, waves and tides?
35. How does the ocean floor look?
36. What elements does ocean water contain?
37. What kinds of life are found in the ocean?
38. What are the earth's resources?
39. What causes air, water, and noise pollution?
40. What are the tools of astronomy?
41. What are constellations?
42. Why is it important to study the stars and outer space?
43. How does a solar or lunar eclipse occur?
44. What is known about the inner and outer planets?
45. Why do the planets circle the sun?

GASES IN THE ATMOSPHERE

Gas	Chemical Symbol	Percentage	Uses
Nitrogen	N_2	78%	used in fertilizers, amino acids, nitroglycerin
Oxygen	O_2	21%	needed by most living things; used as fuel for rockets in its liquid form
Argon	Ar	.94%	used in light bulbs
Carbon dioxide	CO_2	.03%	used by plants in making food
Water vapor	H_2O	0-4%	needed by all living things
Neon	Ne	trace	advertising signs
Helium	He	trace	used in rockets and weather balloons
Methane	CH_4	trace	used in industry, home heating, and gas (for cooking)
Krypton	Kr	trace	used in fluorescent lights
Hydrogen	H_2	trace	used as a fuel; used to cool electric generators and motors; used in the production of ammonia
Xenon	Xe	trace	used to fill flash bulbs
Ozone	O_3	trace	used for disinfecting, cleaning and removing odors

TYPES OF CLOUDS

Name	Description	Weather Prediction
Cumulus	turret-shaped tops, flat bottoms	fair weather
Cumulonimbus	thunderheads (large, dark cumulus)	thunderstorm
Stratus	smooth layers of low clouds	chance of drizzle or snow
Stratocumulus	piles of clouds in layers	chance of drizzle or snow
Nimbostratus	smooth layers of dark gray clouds	continuous precipitation
Altostratus	thick sheet of gray or blue clouds	rain or snow
Altocumulus	piles of clouds in waves	rain or snow
Cirrus	feather-like clouds (made of ice crystals)	fair weather
Cirrostratus	thin sheets of clouds (causes halo around the sun or moon)	rain or snow within 24 hours
Cirrocumulus	"cottony" clouds in waves	fair weather

THE BEAUFORT SCALE OF WIND STRENGTH

Beaufort Number	Description of Wind	Wind Speed (km/hr)	Description
0	calm	less than 1	still; smoke rises vertically and flags hang limp
1	light air	1-5	wind direction shown by smoke drift; weather vanes inactive
2	light breeze	6-11	wind felt on face; leaves move slightly; weather vanes active; smoke does not rise vertically
3	gentle breeze	12-19	leaves and small twigs move constantly; flags blow
4	moderate breeze	20-28	dust and paper blow about; twigs and thin branches move
5	fresh breeze	29-38	small trees sway; white caps form on lakes
6	strong breeze	39-49	large branches move; telegraph wires whistle; umbrellas are hard to hold
7	moderate gale	50-61	large trees sway; it's somewhat difficult to walk
8	fresh gale	61-74	twigs break off of trees; walking against the wind is very difficult; possible damage to property
9	strong gale	75-88	slight damage to buildings; shingles are blown off roof
10	whole gale	89-102	trees are uprooted; much damage to buildings
11	storm	103-117	widespread damage (rarely occurs inland)
12	hurricane	more than 117	extreme destruction

THE CYCLES OF NATURE

The Water Cycle

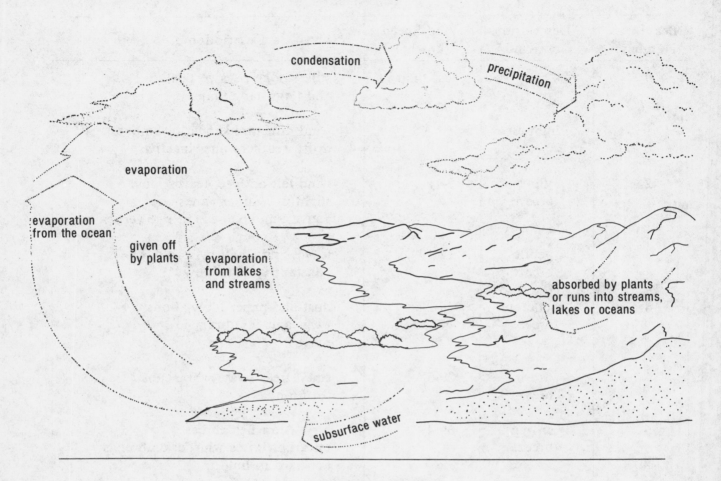

condensation

precipitation

evaporation

evaporation from the ocean

given off by plants

evaporation from lakes and streams

absorbed by plants or runs into streams, lakes or oceans

subsurface water

The Rock Cycle

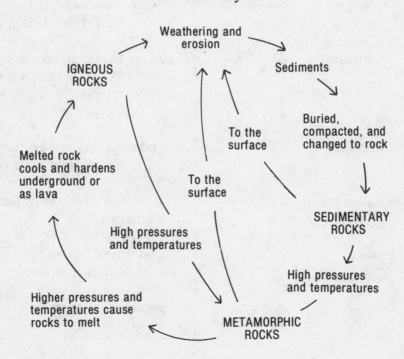

Weathering and erosion

IGNEOUS ROCKS

Sediments

To the surface

Buried, compacted, and changed to rock

Melted rock cools and hardens underground or as lava

To the surface

High pressures and temperatures

SEDIMENTARY ROCKS

High pressures and temperatures

Higher pressures and temperatures cause rocks to melt

METAMORPHIC ROCKS

The Oxygen/Carbon Dioxide Cycle

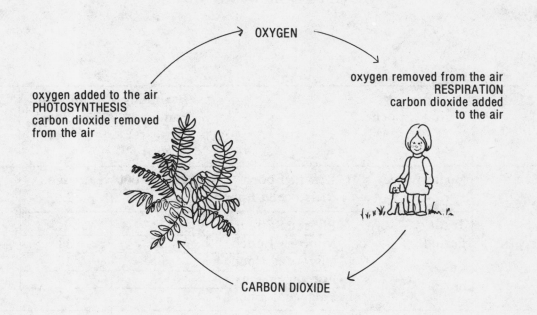

OXYGEN

oxygen removed from the air
RESPIRATION
carbon dioxide added
to the air

oxygen added to the air
PHOTOSYNTHESIS
carbon dioxide removed
from the air

CARBON DIOXIDE

The Nitrogen Cycle

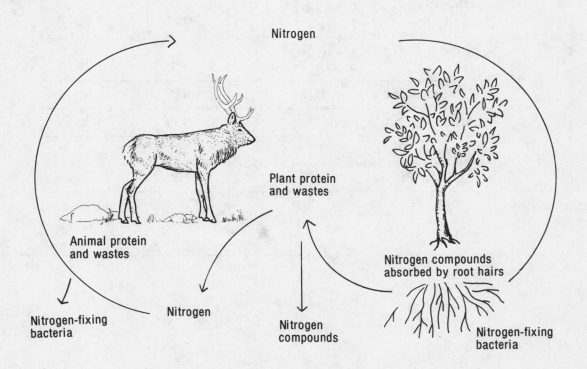

Nitrogen

Plant protein
and wastes

Animal protein
and wastes

Nitrogen compounds
absorbed by root hairs

Nitrogen-fixing
bacteria

Nitrogen

Nitrogen
compounds

Nitrogen-fixing
bacteria

THE GEOLOGIC TIME SCALE

Era	Period/Epoch		Beginning (millions of years) ago)	Duration (millions of years)	Duration of Eras
Cenozoic Era	Quaternary Period	Recent Epoch	began 10,000 years ago		70 million years
		Pleistocene Epoch	2.5	2.5	
	Tertiary Period	Pliocene Epoch	14	11.5	
		Miocene Epoch	25	11	
		Oligocene Epoch	35	10	
		Eocene Epoch	55	20	
		Paleocene Epoch	70	15	
Mesozoic Era	Cretaceous Period		135	65	160 million years
	Jurassic Period		180	45	
	Triassic Period		230	50	
Paleozoic Era	Permian Period		285	55	370 million years
	Carboniferous Period	Pennsylvanian Period	325	40	
		Mississippian Period	350	25	
	Devonian Period		410	60	
	Silurian Period		430	20	
	Ordovician Period		500	70	
	Cambrian Period		600	100	
Precambrian Era			4.6 billion	almost 4 billion years	

BIOME CHARACTERISTICS

Biome	Climate	Common Plants	Common Animals	Average Yearly Rainfall
coniferous forest	cool and moist on mountains; mild winters and heavy rainfalls in coastal areas	conifers: cedars, hemlocks, pines and redwoods	bears, mountain lions, wolves and elks	more than 50 cm
deciduous forest	moist with cold winters and warm summers	broadleaf deciduous trees: elms, maples, oaks	raccoons, squirrels, small birds, deer	more than 75 cm
desert	extremely dry	cacti, fleshy plants, grasses, small-leaved shrubs	lizards, snakes small rodents (wood rats, kangaroo rats)	less than 25 cm
grasslands	mild temperatures and sub-humid	grasses and herbaceous plants	antelopes, buffaloes, wolves, coyotes	25-75 cm
tropical rain forest	warm and wet all year	broadleaf evergreens, palms, tree ferns, climbing vines	bats, lizards, snakes, monkeys, colorful birds	more than 200 cm
tundra	extremely cold and dry; permafrost	lichens, shrubs, grass-like plants	arctic foxes, polar bears, caribou, wolves, migratory birds	20 cm

THE MAKEUP OF THE EARTH

Characteristics of the Earth's Layers

Layer	Chemical Makeup	Average Thickness	Percentage of Total Mass of the Earth
Crust	oxygen, silicone, aluminum, iron, calcium, sodium potassium, magnesium	35 km (continents) 7 km (oceans)	0.4
Mantle	silicone, oxygen, aluminum, iron	2900 km	68.1
Outer Core	iron and nickle (liquid)	2200 km	31.5
Inner Core	iron and nickle (solid)	1270 km	

Elements In The Earth's Crust

Element	Percentage in Crust
Oxygen	46.60
Silicone	27.72
Aluminum	8.13
Iron	5.00
Calcium	3.63
Sodium	2.83
Potassium	2.59
Magnesium	2.09
Titanium	0.04
Hydrogen	0.14
Other	1.23
TOTAL	100.00

Elements In The Ocean

Element	Percentage of Total
Oxygen Hydrogen	96.5
Chlorine	1.9
Sodium	1.1
Magnesium Sulfur Calcium Potassium Bromine Carbon Strontium Silicone Fluorine Aluminum Phosphorus Iodine	0.5
TOTAL	100.0

COMMON MINERALS AND THEIR USES

Mineral	Uses
Alum	used in cosmetics and dyes and also used for purification
Bauxite	a source of aluminum
Calcite	used in medicine and toothpaste; also found in marble and limestone (which are used as building materials)
Corundum	used to make emery boards and to grind and polish metals
Feldspar	used to make pottery, china and glass
Graphite	used in pencils and as a lubricant in small machines, clocks and locks
Halite	rock salt
Hematite	a source of iron
Jade	used to make vases, figurines, jewelry, etc.
Malachite	used to make table tops and jewelry
Quartz	used in radios, televisions, and radar equipment
Sulfur	used to make matches, medicine, rubber and gunpowder
Talc	used to line furnaces, insulate electrical wires, and make powder, crayons, soap and paint

COLOR SORTING KEY FOR MINERALS IN ROCKS

External Color	Streak Test	Mineral
blue-green	white	apatite
blue or white	white	calcite
brass yellow	greenish-black	chalcopyrite
green-purple, white	white	fluorite
lead gray	lead gray	galena
gray, red-brown	red-brown	hematite
brown	orchre yellow	limonite
black	black	magnetite
bright green	pale green	malachite
pale yellow	greenish-black	pyrite
gray or green	white	talc

HARDNESS SCALES

The hardness of a mineral is its ability to resist scratching. A German minerologist named Frederick Mohs developed a scale of hardness for minerals which arranges common minerals according to the hardness of each.

Mohs Hardness Scale

Mineral	Hardness	Hardness Test
Talc	1	softest, can be scratched by your fingernail
Gypsum	2	soft, can also be scratched by fingernail (but not by talc)
Calcite	3	scratched by a penny
Fluorite	4	scratched by a steel knife or a nail file, but not easily
Apatite	5	scratched by a steel knife or a nail file, but not easily
Feldspar	6	knife cannot scratch it, and it can scratch glass
Quartz	7	scratches glass and steel
Topaz	8	can scratch quartz
Corundum	9	can scratch topaz
Diamond	10	can scratch all others

The Field Hardness Scale is helpful for testing hardness when the minerals in the Mohs scale are not available, such as in field work.

Field Hardness Scale

Hardness	Common Test
1	Easily scratched with fingernail
2	Scratched by fingernail (2.5)
3	Scratched by a penny (3)
4	Scratched easily by a knife, but will not scratch glass
5	Difficult to scratch with a knife, barely scratches glass (5.5)
6	Scratched by a steel file (6.5); easily scratches glass
7	Scratches a steel file and glass

CRYSTAL SHAPES

Type	Surfaces	Shapes of Surfaces	Examples
Cubic	6	all are square	alum, pyrite, garnet, gold, sodium chloride, silver, diamond
Hexagonal	8	2 are hexagons 6 are rectangles (angles of rectangles are right angles)	ice, ruby, sapphire, quartz, emerald apatite
Monoclinic	6	4 are rectangles 2 are parallelograms 16 angles are right angles 8 angles are not right angles	sugar, gypsum, borax
Orthorhombic	6	all are rectangles; 3 pairs of rectangles, each pair a different size; corner angles are right angles	topaz, Epsom salt, rhombic sulfur
Rhombohedral	6	all are rhombuses no right angles	calcite
Tetragonal	6	4 are rectangles 2 are squares (corner angles are right angles)	white tin, zircon
Triclinic	6	all are parallelograms (no right angles at corners)	boric acid, copper sulfate

SOLAR SYSTEM STATISTICS

Planet	Average Distance From Sun (millions of km)	Diameter (km)	Period of Revolution (Earth Time)		Rotation (Earth Time)	Moons
			Days	Years		
Mercury	58	4,880	88	-	59 days	0
Venus	108	12,104	225	-	243 days	0
Earth	150	12,756	365	-	24 hours	1
Mars	228	6,787	-	1.88	24.6 hours	2
Jupiter	778	142,800	-	11.86	9.9 hours	16
Saturn	1,427	120,000	-	29.47	10.3 hours	17
Uranus	2,869	51,800	-	84.01	10.7 hours	5
Neptune	4,486	49,500	-	164.8	15 hours	2
Pluto	5,900	6,000	-	248.4	6.4 days	0

PHASES OF THE MOON

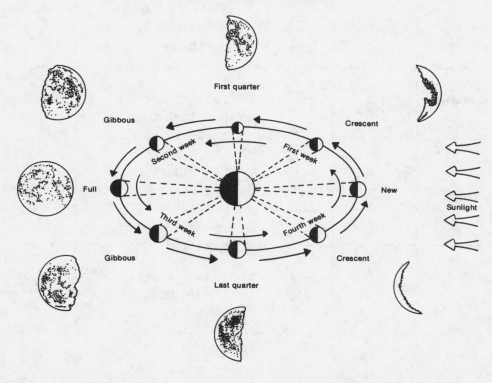

THE NIGHT SKY IN EVERY SEASON

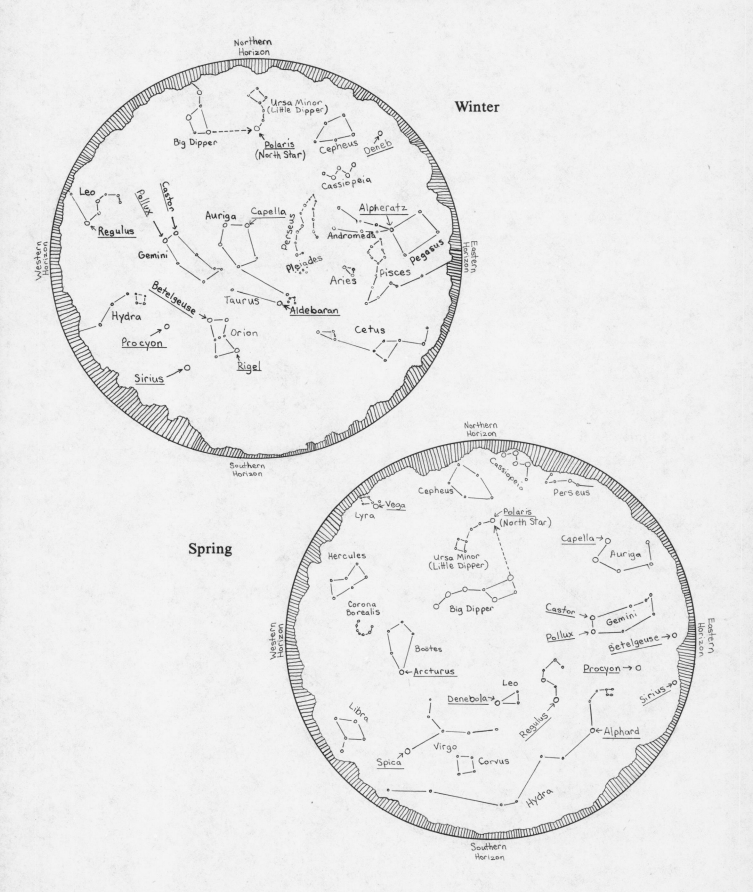

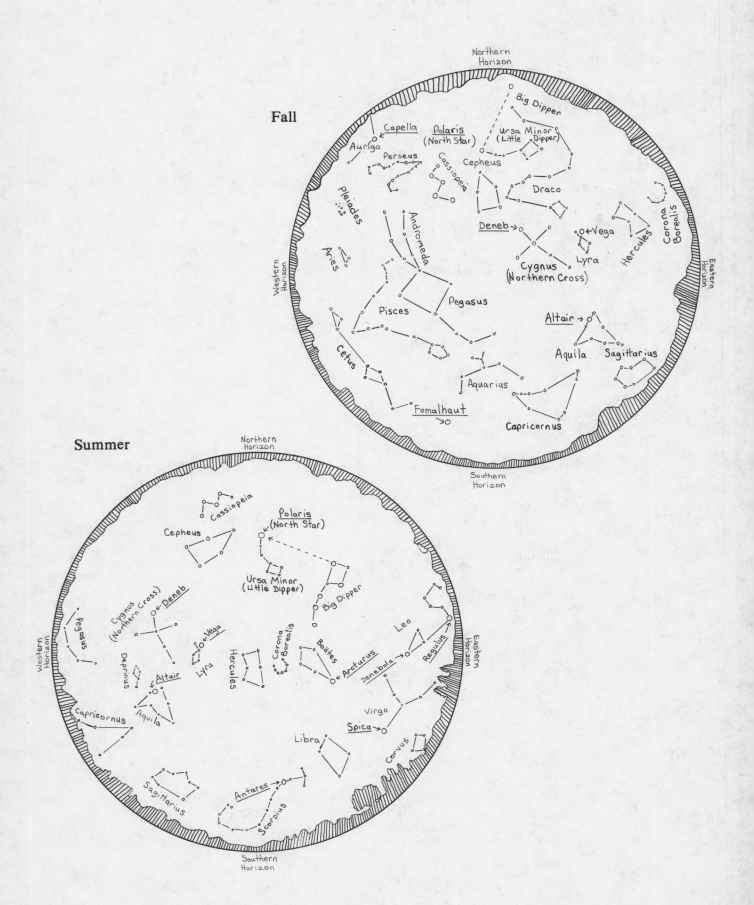

Fall

Summer

EARTH SCIENCE TERMS AND DEFINITIONS

Abrasion - the wearing away of rocks by rubbing and scraping

Anemometer - an instrument used to measure wind speed

Arid Climate - a climate in which the plants receive much less rainfall than they require

Asteroids - numerous small planets with orbits between those of Mars and Jupiter

Astronomy - the study of the stars, planets and other heavenly bodies

Atmosphere - the gaseous mass which surrounds any star or planet

Axis - an imaginary line around which something spins

Cirrus - light and feathery clouds (at heights above 20,000 ft.)

Comet - a heavenly body consisting of rocks and gases which orbits the sun

Conglomerate - sedimentary rock made of pebbles and gravel cemented together by clay

Convection Current - the movement of material within a fluid caused by uneven temperature; the upward movement of warm air and the downward movement of cool air

Density Currents - currents of water that move up and down in the ocean

Desert - a very dry, sandy region

Drag - a force of friction that resists the movement of a body through a fluid medium

Elevation - the distance of a point above or below sea level

Galaxy - a large grouping of millions of stars

Gemstones - a mineral or petrified substance that can be used as a gem when cut and polished

Geologic Time Scale - a history of the earth based on observations of rocks and fossils

Geyser - a spring from which boiling water and steam shoot into the air at intervals

Glacier - a moving river of ice and snow

Gravitational Attraction - the force of attraction that exists between all objects in the universe

Hydrosphere - all of the water on the surface of the earth

Igneous Rocks - rocks formed from the cooling of hot, molten magma

Latitude - distance, measured in degrees, north or south of the equator

Longitude - distance, measured in degrees, east or west of the prime meridian

Lunar Eclipse - the partial or total obscuring of the moon when the earth comes directly between the sun and the moon

Magma - liquid or molten rock deep inside the earth

Mantle - the thick layer of the earth between the crust and the core

Mercury Barometer - an instrument that uses a column of mercury to measure air pressure

Meridian - imaginary lines running from the North Pole to the South Pole

Meteor - the flash of light that occurs when a meteoroid is heated by its entry into the earth's atmosphere (a shooting or falling star)

Meteorite - the part of a meteoroid that passes through the atmosphere and falls to the earth's surface

Meteoroid - any of the small, solid bodies which travel through outer space and are seen as meteors when they enter the earth's atmosphere

Mineral - an inorganic substance which occurs naturally in the earth and has a specific set of physical properties

Mountain - a raised part of the earth's surface with an elevation of at least 600 meters higher than the surrounding land

Orbit - the path of one object in free-fall around another object in space

Period - a subdivision of a geologic era (periods are combined to form eras and are subdivided into epochs)

Phases - any of the recurring stages of changes in the appearance of the moon or a planet

Plain - a large, flat area with an elevation that differs little from that of the surrounding area

Plateau - a large, flat area with at least one side having a sharply higher elevation than that of the surrounding area

Precipitation- the falling of water or ice formed by condensation

Prehistoric - before recorded history

Sandstone - sedimentary rock made of sand

Satellite - a small planet which revolves around a larger one; a man-made object put into orbit around some heavenly body

Schist - a metamorphic rock containing parallel layers of flaky minerals

Sedimentary Rocks - rocks formed by the cementing together of materials

Seismograph - an instrument that measures movements in the earth's crust

Shale - sedimentary rock made of mud and clay which splits easily into thin layers

Sill - igneous rock that has solidified between and parallel to the layers of rock in the earth's crust

Slate - a metamorphic rock that is made from shale and that breaks in flat sheets

Stratosphere - the second layer of the atmosphere (above the troposphere) which extends six to fifteen miles above the earth's surface and where the temperature is fairly constant

Stratus Clouds - clouds that extend in long, low, gray layers

Sunspot - a temporarily cooler area of the sun which appears as a dark spot on the surface

Telescope - an instrument which makes distant objects appear closer and larger

Weathering - the process by which surface rocks and other materials are broken down by wind, water, and ice

Wind - movements of air parallel to the earth's surface

LIFE SCIENCE

STUDENT INVESTIGATIONS

1. Why do living things need air, food, and water?
2. Of what things are living organisms made?
3. What are the major life functions?
4. How do cells, tissues, and organs work together?
5. How do plant cells differ from animal cells?
6. How are living things grouped?
7. How do plants get energy?
8. What is pollination?
9. Why are roots, stems, and leaves important to plants?
10. What parts of plants are sometimes edible?
11. How can a factor of the environment affect growth?
12. What is an ecosystem?
13. How do light, air, water, and temperature affect germination?
14. How is gravity related to growth?
15. What are food chains?
16. What are biomes?
17. Why is it important to balance the environment?
18. How does life continue on earth?
19. How do animals differ from plants?
20. What products are produced from various animals?
21. How do insects develop?
22. Do ants have organized communities?
23. What special adaptations do various plants and animals have for survival?
24. How do various animals take care of their young?
25. What is meant by "survival of the fittest"?
26. How do green plants obtain the necessary materials for photosynthesis?
27. How can one test foods for fat, proteins, and carbohydrates?
28. How does the human eye work?
29. How does the human ear work?
30. How does a tongue taste foods?
31. How does food give the human body energy?
32. What foods contain high amounts of acids?
33. What foods contain high amounts of bases?
34. How can the five senses be "fooled"?
35. What are reflexes?
36. Why is the skin an important sense organ?
37. How do people react to the changes around them?
38. What are inherited characteristics?
39. What is genetic engineering?
40. In what ways can an infection spread?
41. What kinds of bacteria are helpful?
42. What kinds of bacteria are harmful?
43. What is a virus?
44. What is immunization?
45. How do drugs, alcohol, and tobacco affect the body?

THE PARTS OF A FLOWER

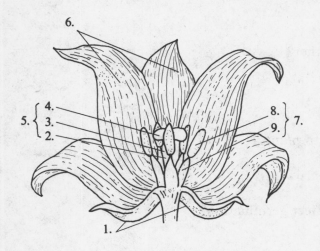

1. Sepals - the outer protective, leaflike parts of the flower
2. Ovary - the enlarged hollow part of the pistil which contains the ovules
3. Style - the slender, stalklike part between the stigma and the ovary
4. Stigma - the free upper tip of the style on which pollen falls and develops
5. Pistil - the seed-bearing organ
6. Petals - the leafy, protective parts of the flower
7. Stamen - a pollen-bearing organ made up of a slender stalk and a pollen sac
8. Anther - the part of the stamen that contains pollen
9. Filament - the stalk of the stamen bearing the anther

THE PARTS OF A PLANT CELL

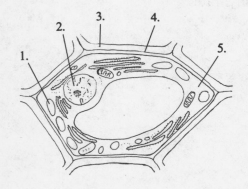

1. Chloroplast - the oval body in a green plant cell which contains the chlorophyll
2. Nucleus - the central mass of protoplasm which contains most of the hereditary material necessary for such functions as growth, reproduction, etc.
3. Cell Wall - the rigid covering of the cell which contains cellulose and other substances
4. Cell Membrane - a very thin living membrane surrounding the cytoplasm
5. Cytoplasm - the protoplasm (essential living matter) of a cell which is found outside the nucleus

COMMON POISONOUS PLANTS

Plant	Dangers
Autumn crocus or meadow saffron	Intense thirst, burning of throat, vomiting; possible death from respiratory failure
Bird of paradise	Severe poisoning if ingested
Black locust	Seeds can cause dullness and depression; vomiting and weak pulse may occur if ingested
Buttercup	Irritant juices may severely injure the digestive system
Crownflower	Sap can cause severe eye injury
Elderberry	Children have been poisoned by using the pithy stems for blowguns; nausea and digestive upset result
Elephant ear	Intense pain around lips, mouth, and tongue if chewed; if base of tongue swells and blocks air passage, death can result
Hyacinth, daffodil, narcissus	Bulbs may cause nausea, vomiting, and diarrhea if ingested; may be fatal
Lily of the valley	Roots, leaves, and fruit can stimulate the heart (similar to digitalis)
Oak	Chewing of leaves or acorns gradually affects kidneys; symptoms appear only after several days or weeks
Philodendron	Skin rash requiring long-term medical care; swelling of mouth and throat if ingested
Red pepper, chili	Burns skin and mouth; large doses may cause severe poisoning
Rhododendron	Intense pain, diarrhea, and discomfort
Rhubarb	Ingestion of large amounts of leaf blades can cause convulsions, coma, and death
Wisteria	Seeds and pods cause mild to severe digestive upset
Yew	Violent gastrointestinal distress; ingestion also causes quick pulse, fainting, convulsions, and death

ANIMAL GROUP AND OFFSPRING NAMES

Animal	Group Name	Offspring
bear	colony	cub
beaver	swarm	kit
cat	flock, cluster	kitten
chicken	clutch, brood	chick
cow	pack, herd	calf
dog	brace, flock, pack, kennel	pup, puppy, whelp
elephant	gang, herd	calf
fox	skulk	cub
goat	cast	kid
goose	flock, gaggle	gosling
hawk	drift	eyas
kangaroo	pride	joey
lion	sord, monkey, pride	cub
pig	drove, litter	piglet, farrow, shoat
rabbit	colony, nest	bunny
seal	pod	pup
sheep	drove, flock	lamb
turkey	rafter	poult
whale	gam, pod	calf
wolf	pack, rout	cub, whelp

SYSTEM OF CLASSIFICATION FOR ORGANISMS

A Swedish scientist named Carolus Linnaeus developed the modern classification system for grouping organisms in the 1700s. This system involves seven classification groups which are (from largest to smallest): kingdom, phylum, class, order, family, genus, and species. This branch of science which deals with classification is called taxonomy.

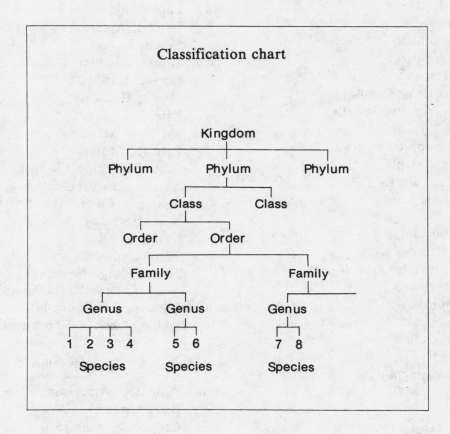

Example: DOG
Kingdom - Animal
Phylum - Chordata
Class - Mammalia
Order - Carnivora
Family - Canidae
Genus - Canis
Species - Canis familiaris

ENDANGERED SPECIES OF NORTH AMERICA AND SELECTED OCEANS

Mammals

Bat, gray
Bat, Indian
Bat, Ozark big-eared
Bear, brown or grizzly
Bear, Himalayan black
Bear, Mexican grizzly
Bison, wood
Bobcat
Caribou, woodland
Chimpanzee, pygmy
Cougar, eastern
Deer, Cedros Island mule
Deer, Columbian white-tailed
Deer, key
Ferret, black-footed
Fox, northern swift
Fox, San Joaquin kit
Gazelle, Mhorr
Jaguar
Manatee, Florida
Mouse, Key Largo cotton
Mouse, salt marsh harvest
Otter, southern sea
Panther, Florida
Prairie dog, Utah
Rhinoceros, Indian
Tiger, Bengal
Tortoise, Galapagos
Turtles, sea
Whale, blue
Whale, bowhead
Whale, finback
Whale, gray
Whale, humpback
Wolf, gray
Wolf, red

Birds

Akepa, Hawaii
Albatross, short-tailed
Blackbird, yellow-shouldered
Bobwhite, masked

Condor, California
Crane, Mississippi sandhill
Crane, whooping
Creeper, Hawaii
Dove, Palau ground
Duck, Hawaiian
Eagle, Greenland white-tailed
Eagle, harpy
Eagle, bald
Falcon, American peregrine
Finch, Laysan
Goose, Aleutian Canada
Goose, Hawaiian
Hawk, Hawaiian
Kite, Everglade
Mallard, Mariana
Pelican, brown
Rail, California Clapper
Shrike, San Clemente loggerhead
Sparrow, Cape Sable Seaside
Stilt, Hawaiian
Stork, wood
Tern, California least
Thrush, large Kauai
Warbler (wood), Bachman's
Woodpecker, ivory-billed
Woodpecker, red-cockaded

Reptiles

Alligator, American
Boa, Mona
Crocodile, American
Gecko, Monito
Iguana, Mona ground
Lizard, blunt-nosed leopard
Lizard, Island night
Rattlesnake, New Mexican ridge-nosed
Snake, Atlantic salt marsh
Snake, eastern indigo
Snake, San Francisco garter
Tortoise, desert
Turtle, green sea
Turtle, loggerhead sea
Turtle, Plymouth red-bellied

DIAGRAMS OF
THE FIVE SENSES

The Ear

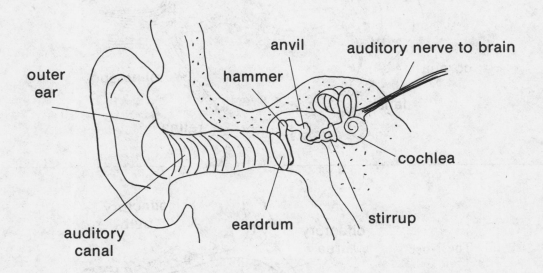

outer ear

anvil

hammer

auditory nerve to brain

cochlea

stirrup

eardrum

auditory canal

The Skin

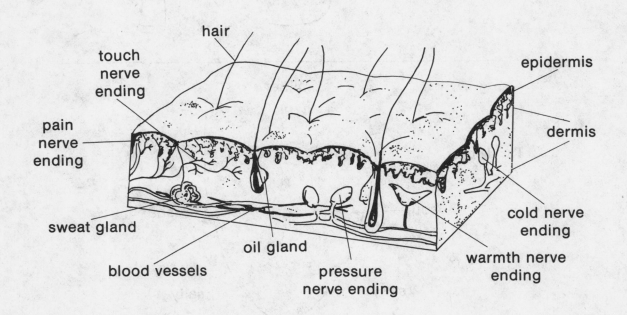

hair

touch nerve ending

epidermis

pain nerve ending

dermis

sweat gland

cold nerve ending

oil gland

warmth nerve ending

blood vessels

pressure nerve ending

The Eye

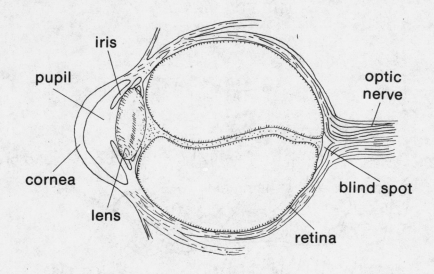

iris

pupil

optic nerve

cornea

lens

blind spot

retina

The Nose

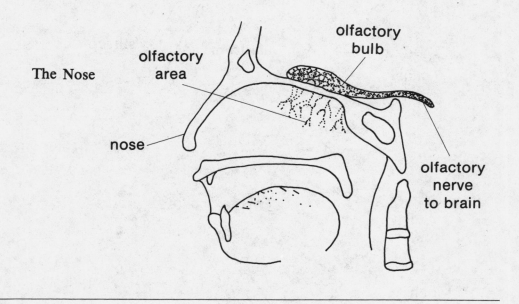

olfactory bulb

olfactory area

nose

olfactory nerve to brain

The Tongue

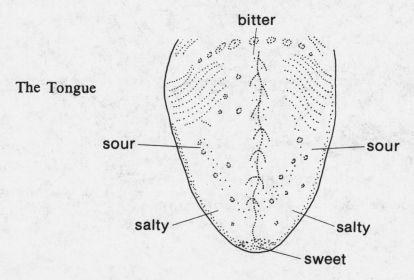

bitter

sour

sour

salty

salty

sweet

THE HUMAN ORGAN SYSTEMS

System	Function
Skeletal	supports and protects the body
Muscular	supports and enables the body to move
Digestive	breaks down food for use by the body
Circulatory	transports food, oxygen, and wastes throughout the body
Respiratory	supplies oxygen to the body and gets rid of carbon dioxide
Excretory	removes wastes from the body
Nervous	carries messages throughout the body to aid in controlling body functions and in responding to the environment
Endocrine	controls various body functions
Reproductive	produces sperm in males and eggs in females
Integumentary (skin)	protects the body

THE PARTS OF AN ANIMAL CELL

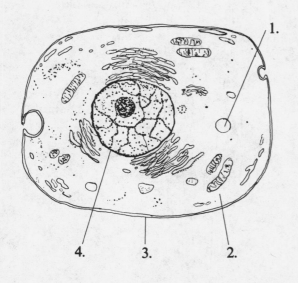

1. Vacuole - a clear, fluid-filled cavity within the plasma membrane believed to discharge excess water or wastes
2. Cytoplasm - the protoplasm (essential living matter) of a cell which is found outside the nucleus
3. Cell Membrane - a very thin living membrane surrounding the cytoplasm
4. Nucleus - the central mass of protoplasm which contains most of the hereditary material necessary for such functions as growth, reproduction, etc.

THE HUMAN SKELETAL STRUCTURE AND BODY SYSTEMS

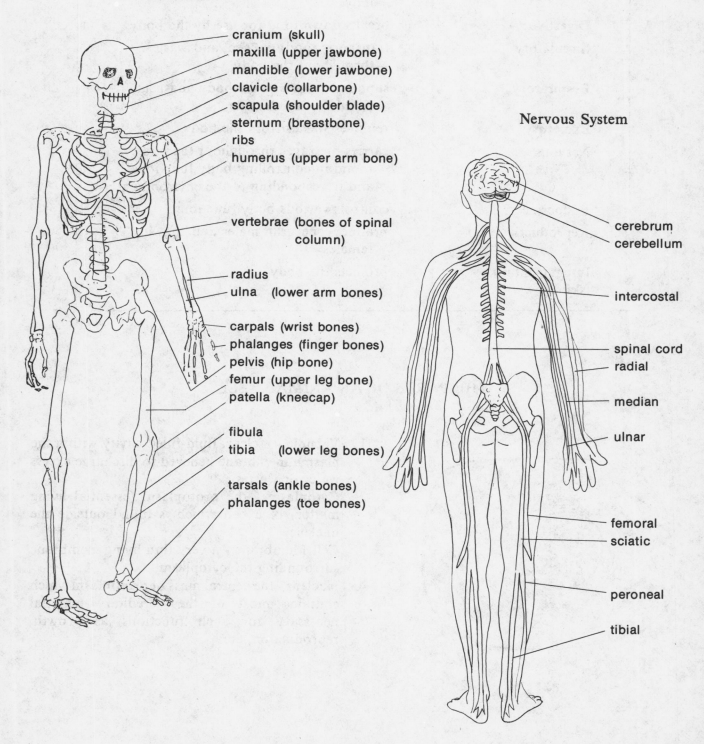

Skeletal Structure

cranium (skull)
maxilla (upper jawbone)
mandible (lower jawbone)
clavicle (collarbone)
scapula (shoulder blade)
sternum (breastbone)
ribs
humerus (upper arm bone)

vertebrae (bones of spinal column)

radius
ulna   (lower arm bones)

carpals (wrist bones)
phalanges (finger bones)
pelvis (hip bone)
femur (upper leg bone)
patella (kneecap)

fibula
tibia   (lower leg bones)

tarsals (ankle bones)
phalanges (toe bones)

Nervous System

cerebrum
cerebellum

intercostal

spinal cord
radial

median

ulnar

femoral
sciatic

peroneal

tibial

Lymph System

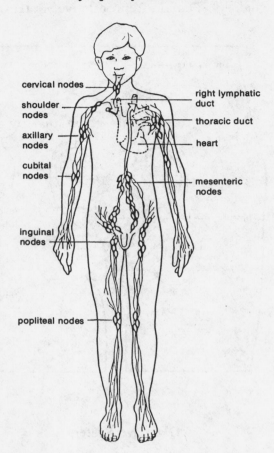

cervical nodes

shoulder nodes

axillary nodes

cubital nodes

inguinal nodes

popliteal nodes

right lymphatic duct

thoracic duct

heart

mesenteric nodes

Endocrine System

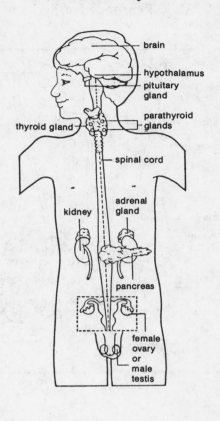

brain

hypothalamus

pituitary gland

parathyroid glands

thyroid gland

spinal cord

kidney

adrenal gland

pancreas

female ovary or male testis

Respiratory System

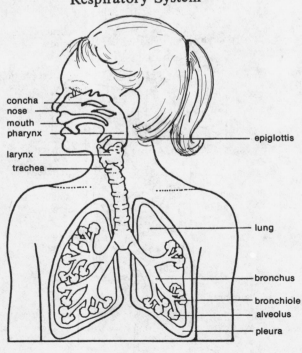

concha
nose
mouth
pharynx

larynx

trachea

epiglottis

lung

bronchus

bronchiole

alveolus

pleura

Circulatory System

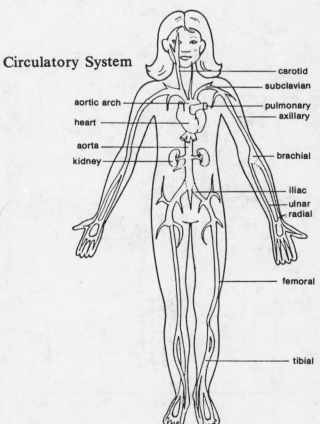

aortic arch

heart

aorta

kidney

carotid

subclavian

pulmonary

axillary

brachial

iliac

ulnar

radial

femoral

tibial

Male Reproductive System

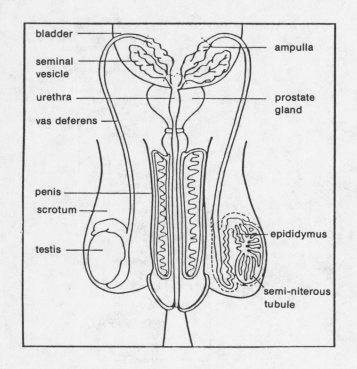

- bladder
- seminal vesicle
- urethra
- vas deferens
- penis
- scrotum
- testis
- ampulla
- prostate gland
- epididymus
- semi-niterous tubule

Female Reproductive System

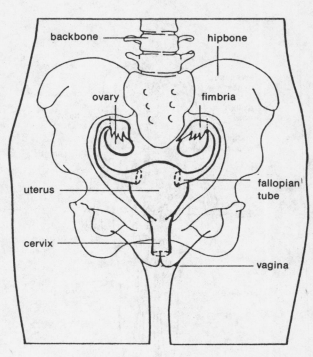

- backbone
- hipbone
- ovary
- fimbria
- uterus
- cervix
- fallopian tube
- vagina

Urinary System

- renal vein
- aorta (artery)
- right kidney
- left kidney
- inferior vena cava (vein)
- right ureter
- left ureter
- bladder
- urethra
- penis

Digestive System

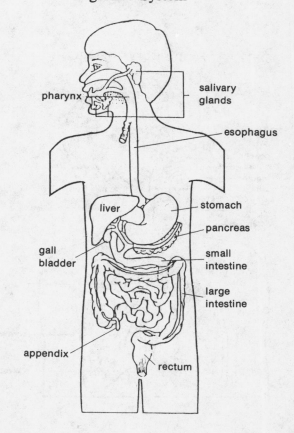

- pharynx
- salivary glands
- esophagus
- liver
- stomach
- pancreas
- gall bladder
- small intestine
- large intestine
- appendix
- rectum

THE FOUR FOOD GROUPS

Milk Group	Fruits and Vegetables	Meat Group	Breads and Cereals
milk, cheese, ice cream, milk chocolate	green and yellow vegetables, oranges, tomatoes	meats, fish, poultry, eggs, beans, nuts	bread, macaroni, cereal

FOOD TESTS

1. **Testing for Protein:** Place a small amount of food in a test tube. Add a small amount of biuret solution. If the solution changes from light blue to purple, protein is present.

2. **Testing for fats:** Rub the food on a piece of a brown paper bag. This will make a spot on the paper. If there are no fats or oils in the food, the spot will not dry but will remain.

3. **Testing for sugar:** Put a small piece of food into a test tube. Pour in enough Benedict's solution to cover the food. Heat the test tube gently. If the solution changes to green, yellow-orange, or brick red, then sugar is present.

4. **Testing for starch:** Add Lugol's solution to the food. If the solution turns blue-black, starch is present.

5. **Testing for water:** Put a small piece of food in a dry test tube. Heat the test tube gently. If the food contains water, the water will be released as vapor. As the vapor touches the cooler surface of the test tube, small drops of water will form inside the tube.

6. **Testing for minerals:** Put a piece of food in a clay dish. Heat the bottom of the dish until the food burns away. If a white or gray ash is left in the dish, the food contains minerals. (Other tests must be done to tell which minerals are left in the ash. Most foods do contain some minerals.)

IMPORTANT VITAMINS AND MINERALS

Vitamin	Food Sources	Needed For
A	green and yellow vegetables, eggs, fruits, liver	maintenance of skin, eggs, and mucous membranes; healthy bones and teeth; growth
B_1	whole-grain cereals, liver and other meats, nuts, vegetables	carbohydrate metabolism; functioning of heart and nerves; growth
B_2	milk, cheese, eggs, liver, fish, fowl, green vegetables	healthy skin; growth; eye functioning; carbohydrate functioning
B_{12}	liver and other meats, eggs, milk, green vegetables	proper development of red blood cells
C	citrus fruits, tomatoes, potatoes, leafy vegetables	healthy bones, teeth, and gums; growth; strength of blood vessels
D	milk, eggs, tuna, liver, sunlight	regulation of calcium and phosphorus metabolism; healthy bones and teeth
E	Milk, butter, vegetable oils	maintenance of cell membranes
K	tomatoes, soybean oil, leafy vegetables, liver	blood clotting; normal liver functioning

Mineral	Food Sources	Needed for
Calcium	milk, eggs	building strong bones and teeth
Iodine	seafood, iodized salt	making a chemical that controls oxidation
Iron	fruits, beans, eggs	building red blood cells
Phosphorus	cheese, meat, cereal	building bones and teeth
Potassium	bananas	keeping muscles and nerves healthy
Sodium	meat, milk, salt	keeping muscles and nerves healthy

CALORIE CHART

Food		Calories
Apple	1 medium	61
Bacon	2 medium slices	86
Banana	1 small	81
Beans:		
baked	½ cup	153
green	½ cup	16
Beef:		
ground, lean	4 oz. raw	186
T-bone steak, broiled	4 oz.	539
Bologna	4 oz.	312
Bread:		
cracked wheat	1 slice (20 per loaf)	60
white	1 slice (26 per loaf)	46
Butter	1 tbsp.	100
Cabbage, white, raw	1 lb.	98
Cake, devil's food with icing	3½ oz. serving	322
Carrots, canned with liquid	½ cup	34
Celery, raw	1-8" outer stalk	7
Cheese:		
American	1 oz.	105
cottage, creamed	½ cup	112
Chicken, roasted with skin	4 oz.	283
Cola	1 cup	112
Cookies, chocolate chip	1 (2¼" diameter)	50
Corn, canned, whole kernels (drained)	½ cup	70
Corn flakes	1 cup	97
Crackers, soda	1 (1 ⅞" square)	13
Cream of wheat, cooked	1 cup	133
Egg:		
boiled or poached	1 large	81
scrambled with 1 tsp. butter	1 large	110
Ham, boiled, packaged	4 oz. (4 slices)	266
Ice cream, 12% fat	½ cup	138
Lettuce, iceberg	1 head (6" diameter)	70
Mayonnaise	1 tbsp.	101
Milk, whole, 3.7% fat	1 cup	161
Orange, navel	1 average	71
Peanuts, roasted	½ cup	421
Popcorn, plain	1 cup	23
Potato chips	10	114
Raisins, seedless	4 oz.	328
Rice, white, long grain	½ cup	112
Sugar, beet or cane	1 tbsp.	46
Tuna, canned in water	4 oz.	144

LIFE SCIENCE TERMS AND DEFINITIONS

Adaptation - a change in structure, function, or form that helps an organism adjust to its environment

Amphibians - the class of vertebrates, including frogs, toads, and salamanders, that begins life in the water as tadpoles with gills and later develop lungs

Angiosperms - a class of plants which includes the flowering plants and which is characterized by having seeds enclosed in ovaries

Antennae - a pair of movable, jointed sense organs on the heads of insects and other related organisms which are used for taste, touch, and smell

Arachnids - the class of arthropods, including spiders and scorpions, which have four pairs of legs, no antennae, and which breathe through lunglike sacs or breathing tubes

Arthropod - the phylum of invertebrate animals with jointed legs and a segmented body such as insects, crustaceans, arachnids, etc.

Bacteria - a group of one-celled, microscopic protists having no chlorophyll and no defined nucleus which multiply by simple division

Benedict's Solution - a blue liquid that is used to test for sugar

Biochemistry - the branch of chemistry that deals with plants and animals and their life processes

Biome - an extensive community of plants and animals whose makeup is determined by soil and climate

Botany - the study of plants

Bulb - an underground plant structure which has roots and which consists of a short stem covered with scales (as in onions and tulips)

Carbohydrate - any of certain nutrients made of sugar or starch

Carbon Dioxide - a colorless, odorless gas that is used by green plants and some protists in photosynthesis and which is given off by all living things in respiration

Chlorophyll - the chemical in chloroplasts of plant cells that is needed for photosynthesis

Chloroplast - an oval structure in the cytoplasm in cells of green plants that contains chlorophyll (photosynthesis takes place in the chloroplasts)

Chromosomes - microscopic, rod-shaped bodies which carry the genes that convey hereditary characteristics and which are consistent in number for each species

Crustaceans - the class of arthropods, including lobsters, crabs, and shrimps, that usually live in the water, breathe through gills, and have a hard outer shell and jointed appendages

DNA - (deoxyribonucleic acid) the acid in chromosomes that carries genetic information

Echinodermata - the phylum of marine animals with a water vascular system and usually a hard, spiny skeleton and radial body (starfishes, sea urchins, etc.)

Ecology - the study of the relationship between plants, animals, and their environment

Ecosystem - a system consisting of a community of animals, plants, and bacteria and its interrelated physical and chemical environment

Fertilization - the joining of nuclei of the male and female reproductive cells

Food Chain - the path of food energy from one organism to another in an ecosystem

Fungi - a kingdom of plantlike organisms which are parasites on living organisms or feed upon dead organic material and which lack true roots, chlorophyll, stems, and leaves, and reproduce by means of spores

Gymnosperms - a large class of seed plants which have the ovules borne on open scales (usually in cones) and which lack true vessels in the woody tissue (pines, spruces, cedars, etc.)

Habitat - the type of environment suitable for an organism; native environment

Heredity - the passing on of traits from parents to offspring by means of genes in the chromosomes

Inherited Traits - traits that are passed on from parents to offspring

Larva - the free-living, immature form of any animal that changes structurally when it becomes an adult (the second stage of insect development)

Mammal - a warm-blooded vertebrate that produces milk to feed its young

Minerals - certain elements essential to the proper functioning of living organisms

Mollusca - the phylum of invertebrates characterized by a soft, unsegmented body (often closed in a shell), and which usually has gills and a foot (oysters, snails, clams, etc.)

Molting - a process by which an animal sheds its outer covering

Nocturnal Animal - an animal active mainly at night

Nucleus - the central mass of protoplasm present in most plant and animal cells which contains the hereditary material and controls the life functions of the cell

Nutrient - a chemical substance found in foods which is necessary for the growth or development of an organism

Offspring - a new organism produced by a living thing

Organ - a group of specialized tissues that work together to perform a special function

Organism - a living thing

Parasite - an organism that lives on or in the body of another organism from which it derives sustenance or protection without benefiting the host and often causing harm

Photosynthesis - the process in which green plants use the sun's energy to produce food

Pollen - the yellow, powderlike male reproductive cells formed in the anther of the stamen of a flower

Pollination - the movement of pollen from a stamen to the upper tip of the pistil of a flower

Protein - any of a large class of nitrogeneous substances consisting of a complex union of amino acids and containing carbon, hydrogen, nitrogen, oxygen, often sulfur and sometimes other elements; proteins are essential for the building and repairing of protoplasm in animals

Protoplasm - the essential living material of all animal and plant cells

Protozoa - the phylum of mostly microscopic animals made up of a single cell or a group of identical cells and living mainly in water (many are parasites)

Sepals - the green, leaflike structures that surround the bottom of flowers

Vertebrates - animals with backbones

Vitamins - organic substances essential for the regulation of the metabolism and normal growth and functioning of the body

Zygote - a cell formed by fertilization